With Wings as Eagles

A novel for young readers

by

William S. Pinkston, Jr.

Bob Jones University Press
Greenville, South Carolina

Illustrated by Dana Thompson
Del Thompson

Cover illustrated by Tim Davis

With Wings as Eagles

©1983 by Bob Jones University Press
Greenville, South Carolina 29614

ISBN 0-89084-231-0

Printed in the United States of America

20   19   18   17   16   15   14   13   12   11   10   9   8   7

Contents

to Jennifer, Ginger, and Jimmy

*"But they that wait upon the Lord
shall renew their strength; they
shall mount up with wings as
eagles . . ."*

Isaiah 40:31

With Wings as Eagles

1 Bob's Birthday

"Happy birthday to you," sang Mrs. Duncan. Bob's mother stood in the kitchen doorway, holding a birthday cake lighted with ten candles.

Dr. Duncan joined in the singing as he reached over and turned out the dining-room light. He then took a brightly wrapped box out from its hiding place on the empty chair.

"Happy birthday, dear Bob," they sang together as they sat the cake and package in front of their son. "Happy birthday to you."

"But it's not my birthday," said Bob in amazement. He almost expected them to realize their mistake, take the cake back to the kitchen, rehide the present, and turn the light back on.

"This is the eighteenth, isn't it?" asked Mom. Bob could tell she was hiding something.

1

"Of course it is," said Dad. "And Bob was born on the eighteenth; I remember that very well."

"But my birthday is the eighteenth of June," said Bob. "This is May."

"What's wrong, son?" asked Dad. "Don't you want to be ten?"

"Sure, but . . ."

"He's concerned about growing old before his time," said Mom with a smile.

"He doesn't need to worry about that until he's my age. Blow out the candles, Bob, before they burn the cake."

Something funny was going on, but Bob didn't want anything to happen to the cake. Already some of the tiny candles had begun to drip wax onto the icing. He blew out the candles. Flash! Dad had taken a picture.

Mom reached over and took the cake. "Now, while I cut this, you open your present."

Bob paused and looked at Dad. He knew his parents were up to something. They knew that his birthday was really in June.

"Go on, open it," said Dad as he turned the lights back on.

Bob tore off the ribbon and the colored paper. He found a plain cardboard box. It gave no clue to what was inside. Dad reached over and, with his pocket knife, slit the tape that held the lid shut. Bob opened the lid and pulled away the tissue paper. Inside was a pair of binoculars.

Bob forgot that it was not his birthday as he pulled the binoculars out of the box. "Oh, wow! Now I won't have to always borrow yours."

"That's why we got them for you," said Dad.

"Now we can both watch the eagles at the same time," said Bob as he put the binoculars to his eyes and looked out the window.

Last summer Bob's father had taught his son to use binoculars. Dr. Duncan was a college professor who taught science during the school year, but during the summer and on weekends he studied a pair of bald eagles that nested near Ward's Lake. Earlier this spring the eagles had returned to their nest. Dr. Duncan had been traveling up to study them almost every weekend since then.

"Can you see anything?" asked Dad.

Bob adjusted the focus knob. "I can see that the paint on the Walker's house number is peeling." He set the binoculars down and looked at his father. "May I take these to Ward's Lake this weekend?"

"Your school class is giving its program on Friday night. And besides, you are signed up to go to the baseball game with your Sunday school class on Saturday," answered Mom.

"May I go with you the weekend after that?"

"We'll see," said Dad.

"Here's your cake," said Mom, removing the box and placing a large piece of chocolate birthday cake in front of Bob.

"Thanks for the binoculars. But it's not really my birthday." It almost didn't seem right having such a wonderful birthday present when his birthday was still a month away.

"We know," said Mom, smiling. "We just

thought we'd celebrate while we were all still together."

Bob frowned. What could that mean?

"We've decided that a ten-year-old is old enough to spend the whole summer with his father at Ward's Lake," said Dad.

"The whole summer?"

"The whole summer. That's why we got you the binoculars. So you won't have to keep waiting for me to finish with mine."

Bob forgot all about the chocolate cake. He could hardly believe that he would be spending the whole summer at Ward's Lake with his father. Bob had spent some weekends with his father at Ward's Lake. And several times each summer Bob and his mother had gone to spend a few days with Dad. But now--a whole summer at Ward's Lake and his own binoculars!

"Can I take the binoculars with me when I go into the woods?"

"Sure," answered Dad.

Bob thought of himself walking along the path that ran through the woods from the A-frame where they stayed to Uncle Joe's cabin. From the path Bob had seen a porcupine and a family of skunks. A stream crossed the path. Near the spot where the stream entered the lake was a waterfall. Sometimes otters played in the waterfall. Bob had always wanted to get a good look at these animals. But whenever he tried to get close to them, they would scamper into the woods and disappear.

Bob had often seen deer tracks along the path, but he had never seen a deer. But with an entire summer to look and with the new binoculars, he was sure to see one this year. He closed his eyes and pictured a deer drinking at the stream. Slowly it lifted its antlered head and turned to look at Bob, who was watching it with his binoculars.

"Well, Jan, do you think our son liked his birthday party?" Dr. Duncan asked his wife as he took a slice of cake.

"I don't know. He's very quiet. Maybe he's disappointed because we didn't put up paper streamers and hang balloons from the light."

"Oh, thank you!" said Bob as his thoughts came back to the dining room. He bounced up and down in his chair. "This is the best birthday I've ever had!"

"Calm down and eat your cake before it gets stale," said Mrs. Duncan with a smile.

2 The Trip

For the next few weeks Bob had a hard time keeping his mind on his schoolwork. He kept thinking about what he was going to do at Ward's Lake during the summer. Finally the day came for them to leave. Bob and Dad packed the car, said good-bye to Mother, and drove off. Soon they were on an expressway headed north.

They had been driving for about an hour and a half when Bob finally spotted what he had been looking for.

"Look, Dad! There they are."

In the distance above the trees they could see the two towers of the Mackinac Bridge. "That's the bridge, all right. It won't be long now."

As the road went down a hill, the towers disappeared behind the trees. It might not seem like a long time to Dad, but Bob knew that Ward's Lake was still far away. But now he could watch the towers grow bigger and bigger as they drove nearer and nearer the bridge.

The five-mile-long Mackinac Bridge connected the mitten-shaped Lower Peninsula of Michigan with the Upper Peninsula. The Duncans lived in the Lower Peninsula, but Ward's Lake was in the Upper Peninsula.

When Bob could see the bridge again, he put his binoculars to his eyes. "Look, Dad! I can see a gull sitting on the cable of the bridge."

"I don't think I should look right now, son. I've got to keep this car on the road. There'll be plenty of time for bird watching later."

For Bob the time went much faster now. Every time he could see the bridge, he looked at it through his binoculars. He watched birds and tried to keep them in sight as they flew. It was not easy. Sometimes he moved the binoculars faster than the birds flew, sometimes slower. Often a bird quickly changed direction, and Bob lost sight of it. He would have to be very good with his binoculars if he expected to see much of Hazel and Ernie. Hazel and Ernie were the names he had given to the eagles at Ward's Lake.

Soon they reached the tip of Michigan's Lower Peninsula. In front of them was the Mackinac Bridge. The middle of the Mackinac Bridge is supported by two thick cables draped over the tops of two five-hundred-foot towers. The road actually hangs from these cables.

As the Duncan's car approached the first tower, Bob tried to look at its top with his binoculars. "Why did the people who built this bridge make it so tall?" he asked.

"They knew that the bridge had to be high enough for large boats to pass under," answered Dad. "So they made the middle of it a suspension bridge."

It was high, all right. When Bob looked at the sailboats and tugboats in the water below, they looked like toys. But when he used his binoculars, he could see people on their decks.

As they left the bridge, Bob focused his binoculars on a sea gull sitting on top of a streetlight. It opened its beak and screeched as if it didn't like being stared at so closely. "They have long pointed tongues in their beaks," Bob observed.

"Who? The gulls? So do Hazel and Ernie," commented Dad.

Soon after they crossed the Mackinac Bridge, Bob and his father left the expressway. They drove on a narrow road that twisted around the hills of Michigan's Upper Peninsula.

Bob began to see places he knew. Ward's Lake could not be far away. They drove by the tiny church they attended when they stayed at Ward's Lake. They passed the hardware store where Dad bought parts for fixing things on the boats or around the cottage. Then Dad pulled off the road at one of the most familiar places, George's Grocery and Bait Shop.

"We'll need some milk for our cereal tomorrow morning," said Dad as he got out of the car. Bob jumped out the other door. His legs felt funny after sitting for so long. He wobbled up the two wooden steps and through the door.

George Collier, the man who owned the store, stood up and folded his newspaper. "Well, well. Good to see you back, Dr. Eagle. I see Eaglet came with you this time."

Dr. Duncan did not seem to mind being called "Dr. Eagle" by some of the people near Ward's Lake. At least if he did, he didn't show it. The nickname did make sense. After all, he was a doctor who studied eagles.

But Bob did not like being called "Eaglet." Baby eagles were ugly. They were all white fluff with big yellow beaks. Grown eagles may like the looks of eaglets, but Bob thought eaglets should stay in the nest until they had real feathers. Usually they did.

"I'll get the milk," said Bob.

"How's business, George?" asked Dr. Duncan.

"I suppose I should be glad to be so busy, but I'm not always sure I like it. I've been so busy today that I haven't read my newspaper yet. Normally I'm done with it by midmorning, but now it's almost closing time and I'm still not finished."

Bob brought the milk to the counter. "Will that be all today, Dr. Eagle?"

"Yes, I think so. Mother sent us off with a good supply of food, didn't she, son?"

Bob remembered the heavy cooler that Mother had packed with frozen casseroles and other homemade food. The entire back seat seemed filled with groceries.

"Your wife didn't come with you this time?" asked Mr. Collier.

"She will be coming up on Thursday afternoon," answered Dad as he paid Mr. Collier. "Then she has to go back home for the weekend, but later she will get to stay longer."

"Too bad she couldn't come up with you for the entire summer. Are you staying with your dad this summer, Eaglet?"

"Yes, sir," answered Bob.

"Why all of this sudden rush of tourists up here?" asked Dr. Duncan.

"They are all fishermen," answered the grocer as he took coins from the cash register. "Last year the biggest northern pike caught in Michigan was taken from Harris Lake. I think everybody who owns a fishing pole in the entire state of Michigan is hoping to catch its big brother this year. Seems like they all stop here to buy bait."

Mr. Collier counted the change into Dr. Duncan's hand. "If things keep going the way they are now, I'll have to hire somebody to help me run this place."

Dad handed the milk to Bob as he put the change in his pocket. "I hope you and your wife will go to church with us some Sunday when Jan is here. Afterwards we could have dinner up at the A-frame," said Dr. Duncan.

"Well, I'm not sure we could. I may have to start opening the store on Sundays just to protect the place. Last Sunday somebody stole my own fishing gear from behind the store. And then yesterday someone tore the locks off the bait tanks and took some bait. It's all those tourists, I'm sure."

"I'm sorry to hear that. I hope it won't get so bad you feel you need to open on Sundays," said Dr. Duncan.

"I hope it doesn't either. Here, Eaglet." Mr. Collier gave Bob a small stick of candy from the jar by the cash register. "Hope you enjoy your stay at Ward's Lake."

"Thank you," said Bob.

Bob and his father got back into the car and started driving down the road.

"Mr. Collier shouldn't open his store on Sunday, should he, Dad?"

"Mr. Collier is not a Christian, Bob. To him Sunday is just a day off, not a day for worship. We need to pray for the Colliers."

Bob thought about this. People who were not Christians didn't seem to understand things sometimes.

3 Ward's Lake

Soon after leaving George's Grocery and Bait Shop, Bob and his dad turned off the road they had been traveling onto a narrower road that disappeared into the woods.

"Look, Dad. They've got the sign up." Bob read the large letters on the dark brown wooden sign: *Welcome to Waunakee National Forest.* He quickly turned around. On the back was *You are now leaving Waunakee National Forest.*

The eleven square miles around Ward's Lake had been purchased by the federal government and added to Waunakee National Forest only three years before. Dr. Duncan said they had wanted the land because it included the Big Pines area on the west end of Ward's Lake.

The pavement ended near the old Smith
farm. The rest of the trip would be on a gravel
road. The Smith family had sold their land so
that it could become part of Waunakee
National Forest. They had moved to a new
farm. Dad said that the Smiths had a better
farm now. But Bob always felt a little sorry for
them when he drove by what used to be their
house. All of the brick had been taken off the
house so that its insides showed outside. The
house always made Bob feel funny.

"Dad! There's somebody in the Smiths'
house. He's watching us through the window."

"Are you sure, son?" asked Dad, slowing down and glancing back. "I don't see anyone."

Bob looked at the window through his binoculars. "I don't either now, I guess. Boy, that place is spooky with its bricks off."

"Well, it won't be there much longer. The Forest Service plans to bulldoze it down in a few days. Then the forest will grow back, and you'll never know the house was ever there."

"Will they do that to our A-frame?"

"It's not really *our* A-frame. The government lets us use it only so that I can study Hazel and Ernie. They won't tear it down until the study is over."

"How long do eagles live?"

"Thirty to forty years sometimes."

"Is that how long you are going to study the eagles?"

"Probably not. The study will continue through this fall at least. I want to continue the study for a few more years, but that is up to the government. Right now the people in the Department of Fish and Wildlife want to know more about bald eagles. That's the reason they pay me to watch Hazel and Ernie."

"But what happens when you find out everything?"

"That's not likely to happen," answered Dad with a smile. "Scientists really don't know too much about bald eagles. What will probably happen is that they will run out of money for this project. Then I will have to stop."

Bob thought of their A-frame looking like the Smiths' house. It was not a pleasant thought. "Will that happen next year?"

"Can't say for sure, Bob. Maybe so, but I hope not." Dr. Duncan glanced at his son. "Don't worry about that, Bob. You have this summer to see that deer."

At that moment they rounded a corner, and there was the A-frame cottage and Ward's Lake. Across the lake the sun was setting. It cast a long trail of dancing lights across the water.

"Here we are," said Dad, turning off the motor. "Isn't it beautiful?"

"Let's go down to the lake. And I want to see Hazel and Ernie. Then may I go and see Uncle Joe?"

"Whoa! Not everything at once. Let's unlock the A-frame, and then go onto the deck and check on Hazel and Ernie. Then we can go down to the lake and check it out. But after that we have to unpack the car and eat supper.

It will be dark soon. Maybe you can go see Joe tomorrow."

Bob ran to the back door of the A-frame. Dad unlocked the door, and they went through the A-frame and slid open the glass doors that led out onto the deck. From the deck they could see about half of Eagle Island, including the dead tree where Hazel and Ernie had their nest. The other half of the island was behind a tree-covered hill.

The eagles' nest was a large platform made of sticks. Sitting on the nest were two bald eagles. Each had its head turned so that one eye faced the deck. They had heard the Duncans come out of the A-frame, and now the eagles were "people watching." Bob always felt a little funny when he knew he was being watched by an eagle.

Bob raised his binoculars and looked back at the eagles. He could see their sharp, curved beaks and their staring eyes. Dad touched Bob's shoulder, and they went back inside and closed the door. "Not too much bird watching tonight," said Dad. "They are ready to go to sleep, but we've got work to do before we can go to bed."

"Let's go down to the lake."

"Okay, but just for a little while," said Dad.

Because of the trees, the eagles could not see the back of the A-frame or the ground around the cottage. Bob and his dad went down to the edge of the lake. Bob breathed deeply of the lake and pine-forest smells. He then turned to look at Eagle Island. From the edge of the lake the whole island was visible. Hazel and Ernie were "people watching" again.

Dad went out onto the dock where he kept a small motorboat and a rowboat. "Looks like somebody must have borrowed the motorboat," said Dad, kneeling on the dock. "That's not the way I tied up the boat."

They started back up the hill toward the A-frame. "Do you think Uncle Joe might have used our boat?" asked Bob.

"We'll ask him. But now we have to unpack the car."

By the time they had taken all the things
from the car to the A-frame, it was dark, and
the stars had begun to show above the hills
across the lake. That night they had a quick
meal of soup and sandwiches. Dad built a fire
in the fireplace while Bob took out the trash.

Bob and his father sat on the floor near the fire and read Isaiah 40 for their devotions. It had been a long day, and Bob was warm and comfortable sitting by the fire. He was almost asleep when they came to the last verse: "But they that wait upon the Lord shall renew their strength; they shall mount up with wings as eagles; they shall run, and not be weary; and they shall walk, and not faint."

Suddenly Bob was awake. What did the verse about the eagles mean? He must have missed something. To him it didn't make sense at all. His father explained. It meant that to those who serve God, God gives the strength they need to do His will.

Then they prayed. They prayed for Mom and that the Lord might use them to be a good testimony to Mr. Collier. Bob went to bed while Dr. Duncan put his telescope together. The eagles would begin their day as soon as it was light, and Dad needed to be ready.

 4 The Eagles

Crash! Bang! Crash!

Bob sat up in bed. It was still dark. Crash! Something was going on outside the cabin.

"Dad! What is it?" asked Bob. "Is it Randal?"

"Probably so," answered Dad from the next room. Randal was the name they had given to the old raccoon that visited their trash can whenever he thought he might find a tasty meal. "Did you fasten the lid when you took out the trash?"

"I'm sure I put the clips on the lid. There was nothing in the trash but crumpled-up newspapers from the boxes Mom had packed. Would Randal open the trash can just for newspaper?" asked Bob.

"What about the soup can?"

Bob had forgotten about the soup can.

"Would Randal get into the trash just for an empty soup can?"

"Randal smells the soup can—he can't tell if it is full or empty until he gets it." There were muffled noises from outside. "Are you sure you put the clips on the lid?"

"Yes, sir," answered Bob. "He must have figured out how to get them off."

"That's strange. In any case, you are probably going to have some newspapers to pick up tomorrow morning."

Bob did not answer. He was sure he had fastened the lid of the trash can. Picking up paper! What a dumb way to spend the first morning of your first whole summer in the woods. As things grew quiet outside, he drifted off to sleep.

When Bob woke up again, light was streaming in the window. He got out of bed, dressed quickly, and put the strap of his binoculars around his neck. Dad was already out on the deck looking through the telescope at the eagles' nest. Bob stuck his head out the front door. "'Morning, Dad," he whispered.

Dad smiled at Bob and then wrote something in his field book. The field book was where he kept a record of what Hazel and Ernie did. Bob could see an eagle on the nest. He focused his binoculars on the eagles' nest, trying to bring the eagles into view.

Bob could tell the difference between Hazel and Ernie if he saw them together. Hazel was much larger than Ernie. Dad told him that it was normal for the male eagle to be smaller than the female. But without both eagles at the nest, Bob could not tell which one was looking back at him. "Is that Hazel or Ernie? And why is he, or she, sitting so funny?"

"That's Hazel. And she's sitting on two eggs."

Normally the parent eagles take turns sitting on their eggs, keeping them warm for about thirty to forty days. Then tiny eaglets hatch. But last year Hazel's eggs had not hatched. Long after the eggs should have hatched, Dr. Duncan and two of his students climbed the tree and took the eggs.

Dr. Duncan had studied the eggs carefully. He decided that Hazel probably had not laid eggs before. Since Hazel was a young eagle, it was not surprising that her first eggs might not have baby eagles in them. But everyone had been sad that they had not hatched.

"Will the eggs hatch this year?" asked Bob.

"I hope so. But you never know."

Bob looked at Hazel and thought about the eggs under her. Then the eagle stood up and started pushing the eggs around. "Dad, what's she doing?" asked Bob in alarm.

"Just turning over her eggs."

The action looked a bit rough to Bob. He would never handle eggs that way. "She won't break them, will she? They won't roll off the nest or anything?"

Dad smiled. "Probably not. The eggs are in a bowl-shaped place in the center of all those branches and twigs." He looked over the lake with his binoculars. "Well, look who's coming."

Bob focused his binoculars on the bird that was coming across the lake. "Is that Ernie?"

"Sure is, and looks like he's got breakfast with him."

Bob was having a hard time keeping the eagle in his sight. He should have practiced more on those gulls. Bob saw nothing in Ernie's beak. "Where's breakfast?"

"Look in his talons. He holds them back against his tail when he flies. Looks like he's got a fish."

The eagle was much closer now, and Bob could just begin to see something in the bird's

strong feet. Ernie swooped down and landed
on the nest. Dad was looking through the
telescope. "Not bad fishing, Ernie. Looks like
a good-sized trout."

Bob looked at the fish Ernie was holding in
his talon. Hazel was looking at the fish too.

"Now to see if he shares or if Hazel has to
go get something to eat herself," said Dad as he
wrote in his field book. Bob and his father
watched. Ernie did share. In fact he let Hazel
eat some pieces of meat he ripped off. But after
the fish was gone, Hazel flew off across the
lake and out of sight, and Ernie settled himself
on the eggs.

Dad and Bob decided it was time for their breakfast. But Dad needed to stay on the deck to see if Hazel brought anything back. He sent Bob inside to prepare two bowls of dry cereal and get two oranges.

When Bob came back out on the deck, he found a small package at his place on the table. "This is the rest of your birthday present. But I think you will need to open this early too."

Bob ripped off the paper. He found a small black notebook just like Dr. Duncan's field book. On the cover, in the lower right-hand corner, were the words:

Field Book
Bob Duncan

Inside were blank paper and a tiny pocket which held a small pencil.

"Now I can write down what I see," said Bob with a big smile. He took the pencil, wrote the date, the time, and the word *deck*. He knew that all of these facts were important because he had read his father's field book many times. Then he wrote: "Ernie brought a good-sized trout for breakfast. Both ate it. Hazel then left nest. Ernie sat on eggs."

"Now you had better eat your cereal before it gets too soggy."

"Can I write down about all the animals I see?"

"That's what you are supposed to do. And I want to read what you write on the day you see that deer," said Dr. Duncan, finishing his cereal.

Bob ate his breakfast.

"That should keep us until lunch," said Dad. "But now, don't you have some cleaning up to do?"

Bob gave his father a questioning look.

"Remember Randal and the newspaper? Look." Dad pointed down the hill.

Bob looked over the railing of the deck. On the ground below he saw the torn-up newspaper. It was scattered all the way down to the lake.

"But won't I disturb the eagles if I go out there?" asked Bob hopefully.

"They can't see you when you are on the ground on that side of the A-frame. As long as you are quiet and don't run around too much, they won't mind." Then Dad grinned. "Besides, you wouldn't want Ranger Peak to come and see that mess, would you? He'd probably kick us out of the national forest for littering. As soon as I find out what Hazel is doing, I'll come and help."

Bob got a large plastic bag and started picking up the newspaper. On the rock beside the trash can were the lid clips. Maybe Bob *had* forgotten to put them on the lid. No, he remembered putting them on. But if Randal or his raccoon friends had taken them off, they would be scattered, not lying neatly on the rock.

There were hundreds of raccoon tracks all around. "They must have had a good time out here last night," thought Bob as he started picking up the newspapers.

After a while Dad came out the back door. He looked on the back porch. "Bob, did you move the cooler?"

"No, sir, I put it on the back porch last night, just like you told me."

"Well, it's not here now."

"Do you think Randal and his raccoon friends might have taken it? It might have smelled good."

"They wouldn't *take* it. Humm." Dad was looking at the ground near the edge of the porch. Bob came over to see what he was looking at. "If Randal took the cooler, he's started wearing tennis shoes," said Dad.

Bob looked at the tennis-shoe tracks beside the porch. "Those aren't Randal's tracks. They're mine."

"I don't think so, son. Your foot is too small to make that track. And I wasn't wearing tennis shoes yesterday."

"And here are some tracks on the porch— right where I put the cooler."

"Well, son. It looks like somebody stole our cooler."

Bob went over to the trash can. "Look, Dad, there are big tennis-shoe tracks here too. Do you think the person who stole the cooler may have taken the clips off the trash can too?"

"Maybe so," said Dad, looking toward the road.

"Maybe it's the same person who borrowed our boat?"

"Maybe," answered Dad.

"But who? We're the only people around here, except for Uncle Joe. And he always wears boots."

"Well, it appears that there's somebody else here too."

5 Uncle Joe

"May I go see Uncle Joe?" asked Bob, as he finished lunch.

"Sure, if he's home." Dad went to the radio, picked up the microphone, and pushed the button on its side. "Calling Beaver Watch. This is Eagle Watch calling Beaver Watch. Come in Beaver Watch."

Uncle Joe was not really Bob's uncle, nor was he studying beavers like Dr. Duncan was studying eagles. His real name was Joseph Ward, and he was old enough to be Bob's grandfather. Uncle Joe called Bob "young man," or "sonny," but never "Eaglet." Ward's Lake had been named after Uncle Joe's great-grandfather. He had owned all the land around the lake. But that was long ago.

"Calling Beaver Watch. This is Eagle Watch. Come in Beaver Watch." Bob and his father waited a moment. Then they heard Uncle Joe's voice over the radio.

"Hello Eagle Watch. Beaver Watch here. Glad you're back in the neighborhood. Over."

"Glad to be up here," said Dr. Duncan into the microphone. "I have a young man here who'd like to ask you something. Hold on."

Dad gave the microphone to Bob. Bob pushed the button on its side and spoke, "Uncle Joe, may I come over and see how you and the beavers are doing? Over."

"Well, hello, young man. Sure. Come on over," said Uncle Joe. "The ice was a little hard on the beavers' dam last winter. They've been fixing it for the past few days. I was planning to go over and see how they were doing this afternoon. Having a little company would be real nice. Over."

Bob smiled at his father and gave him the microphone. "I'll drive Bob up your way in a few minutes," said Dr. Duncan into the microphone. Bob frowned. Did Dad think that Bob had forgotten the way to Uncle Joe's?

"We had a prowler up here last night, and I think I'd better not let Bob walk over alone.

How about coming back with him this evening and having supper with us? Jan made one of those chicken-and-squash casseroles you like so well and sent it up with us. She told me to make sure you came over for supper the night we had it. So if you don't have other plans, how about it? Over."

"Me have other plans? Ha! And don't think I'd turn down a chance at one of your wife's casseroles. By the way, does your prowler wear tennis shoes? Over."

Bob and his father looked at each other. "Yes. Do you know who he is? Over."

"No. I just know that some things have been missing and that someone in tennis shoes has been around here for a little over a week now. I caught a glimpse of him a few days ago. That's about all I know. Over."

"Well, we can talk about it over supper. I'll bring Bob over in a few minutes. Eagle Watch over and out."

"I'll be waiting for you. Beaver Watch out."

After hearing what Uncle Joe had said, Bob did not feel so bad about his father's driving him to Uncle Joe's log cabin. Uncle Joe's grandfather had cut down the trees and fitted them together to build that cabin over one hundred years ago. When the cabin was first built, it had only one room. Now that room served as the living and dining room. Several bedrooms, a kitchen, and a bathroom had been added to the cabin.

Bob enjoyed hearing Uncle Joe tell about what it was like when he was Bob's age. Uncle Joe could show you the bucket he had used to "fetch water" from the spring when he was a boy. He could remember when his log cabin had to be lit by kerosene lamps because they didn't have electricity yet. He could even show you the room in his log cabin in which he had been born.

When the government was buying the land around Ward's Lake to add to the Waunakee National Forest, it bought the land that Uncle Joe owned. But he did not want to leave the cabin he had lived in all his life. So the people who ran the National Forest Service gave him permission to live in his log cabin as long as he wanted to.

Uncle Joe was standing outside when Dr. Duncan drove up with Bob. The boy jumped out of the car and ran down the path to Uncle Joe. "Hi! Dad says to tell you that supper is at six."

"At six, eh? Fine. That will give us plenty of time to see what those beavers are doing."

"Let's go and get a drink of water, and then let's go see the beavers. I want to watch them with my binoculars."

"Got yourself some binoculars, eh?" asked Uncle Joe. "You ought to be able to see what they are doing real well with those."

"You can use them too if you want to."

"Why, thank you, sonny," said Uncle Joe, smiling. "I've always wanted to get a good close look at those beavers."

They walked to a tiny spring near the log cabin. The water gushed out from the spot at which two rocks met and then fell a few inches into a pool which was the beginning of a tiny stream.

Bob dashed ahead to the place where Uncle Joe kept a dipper hanging on a tree. The dipper was used to catch the spring water for drinking. The nail was empty.

"Where's the dipper?"

"One morning it was gone. By all the tennis-shoe tracks I found, I'd say that prowler took it." Uncle Joe cupped his hands together. "Just lean over and cup your hands like this. Then sip the water from your hands. Water tastes just as good from your hands as it does from a dipper."

More water ran down the front of Bob's shirt than got into his mouth. "If your hands have holes in them, you need to lean over more," said Uncle Joe, smiling. After a couple of tries, Bob was able to satisfy his thirst. The water from the spring flowed in a tiny stream down the hill to Big Rib Creek. The creek rounded the base of the hill on which Uncle Joe's cabin was built. It was on Big Rib Creek that the beavers had built their dam. The water of Big Rib Creek had then filled in between two hills, forming a beaver pond.

As Bob and Uncle Joe went around the edge of the pond, they could see signs of beaver activity. Wood chips surrounded pointed tree stumps. Where the beavers had pulled branches, there were trails. These trails led into the pond.

"This beaver dam is older than my cabin," said Uncle Joe. "Every spring they fix up any-thing that might be wrong with it."

Bob could see some of the work they had done this year. A few of the fresh branches still had leaves on them.

In the middle of the pond were three mounds of branches and dirt called lodges. The beavers lived in these lodges. Their entrance ways were underwater, but the beavers lived in dry rooms above the water level. Bob wished his binoculars would let him see inside the lodges. But they couldn't.

No beavers would show themselves as long as Uncle Joe and Bob were so close and so noisy. They climbed a little way up one of the hills and selected a spot where they could see all the pond. They sat down and quietly watched for the first beaver to come out of the pond.

Shortly a small, wet, furry body waddled up out of the water and sat up. Holding its front paws in tiny fists close to its body, the beaver looked around and sniffed. Bob grabbed his binoculars and nudged Uncle Joe. The movement caught the beaver's attention, and it looked toward Bob and Uncle Joe. They both sat very still. Beavers cannot see things at a distance very well. Since there was no more movement, the beaver decided that nothing was wrong and went on about its business.

The beaver waddled up onto the shore, dragging its flat, leathery tail behind it. It went to a bush and started gnawing. Bob watched its sharp, orange teeth quickly cut off chips of wood. Soon the bush was down, and the beaver began pulling it toward the water. Before long several beavers were busily gnawing other small trees around the pond. Uncle Joe and Bob spent most of the afternoon passing the binoculars back and forth, watching the beavers. Bob wrote notes in his field book.

Splash! Splash! A beaver on the far side of the pond began slapping his tail against the water. It was their warning signal. Something had frightened them. There was a scurry of activity as all the beavers slid into the water.

"Why did they do that?" asked Bob after the last beaver was gone.

Uncle Joe was using the binoculars to look at the top of the hill across the pond. Bob looked at the same place just in time to see a blond-haired person disappear behind the hill.

"Who was that?" asked Bob.

Uncle Joe took the binoculars from his eyes. "I don't know. But I think I've seen him somewhere before."

"Is he the prowler? Did he have on tennis shoes?"

"I didn't see his feet. But I think he's the person who's been around here for the past week or so."

Later Uncle Joe and Bob walked along the gravel road back to the A-frame. At supper that evening Bob told his dad about seeing the prowler.

"What else can you tell me about this guy, Joe?" asked Dr. Duncan.

"Well, not much. He's been around here for a week or so now, judging from when I first noticed his tracks. I'm pretty sure he's been taking things. At first I thought I'd just mislaid them. But his tracks were always around the place where the thing I couldn't find was supposed to be. So I started making sure that things were in the shed and that the shed was locked."

"What sort of things has he been taking?"
asked Dr. Duncan.

"He took the dipper off the tree by the
spring," answered Bob.

"The dipper," said Uncle Joe, "and my little
hatchet. He took my small shovel, some jars,
and the knife I kept in the shed. Once when I
came back from fishing, I was pretty sure he'd
been in my cabin. Some cans of soup and
beans were missing."

"Have you seen him any other times?" asked
Dr. Duncan.

"Not up close. I think I saw him off behind
some bushes. Another time I saw him dashing
across the road," answered Uncle Joe. "After I
saw him with Bob's binoculars today, I was
sure I recognized him from somewhere, but I
just can't remember where."

"What's he look like?" asked Dr. Duncan.

"Well, to me he looks like a teenage kid.
He's taller than you are, but he's skinny, real
skinny. And he's got blond hair."

"Have you told Ranger Peak about this?"
asked Dr. Duncan.

"Plan to next time he's out this way,"
answered Uncle Joe. "He probably will be
soon. He hasn't been here for a couple of weeks
now."

They finished their meal and talked about eagles and beavers for a while. Then Dad offered to drive Uncle Joe back to his cabin. As Bob opened the back door, he switched on the back light. "Dad, look!" Bob pointed toward the gravel drive.

Dad and Uncle Joe saw the back of a blond-haired teenager running toward the road. He turned his head and glanced back at the A-frame. Then he ran into the woods and disappeared into the darkness.

"Dad, catch him!"

6 Ranger Peak

Bob and his father drove Uncle Joe to his log cabin, and then returned to the A-frame. As they drove up to the A-frame, Bob looked carefully into the darkness for any sign of the prowler they had seen earlier. "You won't see any more of him tonight," said Dad. "He's probably a mile and a half away from here by now."

"How old would you say he is?" asked Bob.

"I don't know—maybe fourteen or fifteen."

"Where do you think he lives?"

"I guess that he's staying in the woods somewhere."

"Why is he living alone in the woods?"

"I don't know, son."

After their time of Bible reading that night, they both prayed for the prowler. Bob prayed for his safety and that the Lord would help him while he was in the woods. Dad prayed for his special needs and that the Lord would possibly use them to help him.

After prayer Bob suggested, "We could help meet his special needs by leaving food out for him, couldn't we?"

"Yes, he probably needs food," answered Dad, looking out the window. "But he must have other needs that are much bigger than his need for food. Whatever is causing him to live out there in the woods must be really important to him." Dad stood up and smiled at Bob. "Besides, if we left food for him, Randal and his friends would get it long before that fellow got it. Time for bed now."

The next morning when Bob woke up, his father was again on the deck watching Hazel and Ernie. Bob stuck his head out the door. "Ready for breakfast?" he whispered.

Dad nodded, and Bob went to fix two bowls of cereal, several slices of toast and jelly, and two glasses of orange juice. Again they ate on the deck, watching the two bald eagles. The eagles had rabbit for breakfast.

Bob looked at Hazel and Ernie through his binoculars. "Dad, how can you be sure that these are the same eagles that were here last year?"

"When you have studied as many eagles as I have, you begin to see differences in them just as you see differences in people. I could recognize those two eagles anywhere."

Bob looked at them again. Except for their size, they looked just alike to him. And they looked just like the bald eagle he had seen in a zoo last summer and just like all the pictures of bald eagles he had ever seen. "Will they always come here to Ward's Lake?"

"Eagles usually stay with the same mate until one or the other of them dies. And usually once they have found a good nesting place, they use it again and again if nothing goes wrong."

"What could go wrong?"

"Usually it's that people move into the area. Eagles will stay if there are a few quiet people in their territory. But building a city or even having a lot of noisy farming in the area will cause the eagles to leave."

Dad paused to write something in his field book. "The nest that Hazel and Ernie are using was built by other eagles some time ago. I'm not sure what caused the eagles that were using it before to leave. It may have been the building of this A-frame that scared them off. I'm sure they did not like a lot of motorboats on the lake. The farming at the Smiths' place probably did not appeal to them either. But when the government bought the land, everything got quiet again. That's when Hazel and Ernie moved in."

The eagles held their heads high and looked behind the A-frame. "There's probably something on the road. They caught sight of it through the trees," said Dad.

"Could it be the prowler?"

"Not unless he's got a car today. Listen." Bob could hear the sound of wheels on a gravel road. "Go and see if you recognize who drives by," said Dad.

Bob went to the back of the A-frame but was back quickly. "He didn't drive by. It's Ranger Peak, and he's coming here."

"Good. Tell him I'll be there as soon as I write down some notes."

By the time Bob got to the back door, Ranger Peak was out of his brown National Forest Service truck and almost to the door. He wore jeans and a plaid shirt. Hanging from his shirt pocket was a plastic badge which had his picture and his name, *Ranger Dick Peak*, on it.

"Hi!" said Bob, coming out of the door.

"Well, hi, Bob." Ranger Peak did not call Bob "Eaglet" either.

"Dad's writing down some notes. He'll be here in a minute."

Ranger Peak's coming usually meant good times at the A-frame. Dick Peak and Dr. Duncan had grown up together in Catawba, a small town about thirty miles away.

When Dr. Duncan came out of the A-frame, the two men shook hands, and then talked while Bob listened. Bob liked to listen to them. They knew just about everything about the woods. Bob hoped they would talk about the woods so that he could learn some things. But, as sometimes happened, today they were talking about things back in Catawba. Bob kicked at the gravel in the driveway as he leaned against the truck.

"Did you know that Ralph Howard died a couple of months back?" asked Ranger Peak.

"No. I'm sorry to hear that," said Dad.

"Ralph used to come deer hunting up here," said Ranger Peak.

Bob knew that people went deer hunting. But suddenly he was concerned about the deer whose tracks he had seen in the woods last year. "Did they ever kill a deer up here?" asked Bob.

"You'd have to ask Joe Ward about that," answered Ranger Peak. "Ralph hunted here when the land belonged to Joe."

"No one has hunted in this area since it was set aside for the eagle study," explained Dad. "At least they haven't if Dick's been doing his job," he added with a smile.

Bob felt much better. His deer was probably still out there. Maybe Dad would let him go and try to find it later today. Bob went back to kicking gravel.

Ranger Peak leaned back on his truck and said, "The reason I came was to tell you that I have seen some eagles on the other side of the Big Pines. Haven't seen a nest or anything, but thought you would like to know."

"I'd better go over and have a look," said Dr. Duncan. "That's far enough away that Hazel and Ernie would probably not consider them in their territory. I hope we won't have any territory fights. Maybe those you saw were just passing through."

"Could be," answered Ranger Peak.

"Now, we've got some things to tell you. Seems we have a prowler around here," said Dad. Ranger Peak began to look serious. He took a note pad out of his pocket and wrote notes as Dr. Duncan told him what had been happening.

"I'd better go over to Joe's place and see if he can tell me anything else," said Ranger Peak.

"No idea who this prowler might be?" asked Dad.

"Nothing has come through the office that I have seen that would give a clue," answered Ranger Peak as he opened the door of his truck.

"Jan's coming up day after tomorrow, bringing along one of my students who's been studying the water in the lake. How about you and your wife coming over for supper on Thursday night?" asked Dad.

"We can't on Thursday. Maybe sometime later?" asked the ranger as he got into his truck.

"Sure. We'll set up a time," said Dad, smiling.

"And you keep an eye on these people you have up here, Dan," cautioned Ranger Peak. "Call on Joe at least once a day. Prowlers in the woods make me nervous."

"Don't worry too much about old Joe. He can take care of himself. But I'll keep my eyes open. And you'll let me know if anything turns up about this prowler, right?"

"Sure. Take care. And call me on the radio if anything happens," said Ranger Peak as he started the engine.

"Sure will. See you."

Ranger Peak smiled and nodded as he drove off toward Uncle Joe's cabin.

7 The Big Pines

Dr. Duncan led his son into the A-frame, opened a drawer, and took out two whistles on long braided loops. "Here, son, put this around your neck." He put the other whistle around his own neck. "I don't think our prowler will be around in the daylight, but I want you to wear this just in case. If you ever see anybody you don't know, you are to blow the whistle as loud as you can and keep blowing it. Do you understand?"

"Yes, sir."

"As soon as you blow your whistle, I'll come running. And you start running toward the A-frame as you blow it."

"Yes, sir. And if you see him, you are going to blow your whistle, and I'll come."

Dad smiled. "Not exactly. When I blow my whistle, you are to give me a short whistle back to let me know that everything is all right."

"Oh," said Bob, a little disappointed. He looked at the shiny whistle.

"Now for the hard part. Unless I'm with you, I don't want you to go anywhere you can't see the A-frame."

Bob looked up at his father with disbelief in his eyes. With so many trees nearby he could go hardly anywhere without losing sight of the A-frame. What good was being at a cottage in the woods if you couldn't go into the woods?

"But Dad, what about looking for animals and writing in my field book?"

"You will have to be content with watching Hazel and Ernie and with what you can see around here."

"But, Dad—"

Dad knelt down so that he was eye to eye with Bob. He took his son by the shoulders. "Bob, I know you are disappointed. I am too. But we can't take chances. A prowler is out there somewhere, and we don't know what kind of person he is or what he wants. So I want you to stay near the A-frame. Do you understand?"

Bob looked down at the floor. "Yes, sir," he muttered.

"Now let's go out on the deck and see what Hazel and Ernie are doing. You know, Bob, sometimes when I've been on the deck I've seen a whole deer family," said Dad as he headed for the deck.

"Where?"

"They come and take a drink of water on that little point of land across the lake. It wouldn't be like seeing your deer close up in the woods, but you could use your binoculars. And it would be something to write in your field book."

Bob and his dad went out onto the deck. Dad watched the eagles and recorded things in his field book. Bob watched the eagles for a while, but they didn't seem to be doing anything. Bob looked all around the lake with his binoculars. Then he began to think about the prowler.

At first the thought of having a prowler around had been exciting, even fun. Then Bob felt angry and hurt and sorry for himself. Next he decided he should feel sorry for the prowler. The more Bob thought about it, the less certain he was how he should feel. One thing was for sure: he wished the prowler would go away.

Things were going to get pretty boring if Bob had to stay around the A-frame all the time. Mom and Dad's student, Stuart McGregor, would arrive tomorrow. Bob would then spend most of Friday with Stuart. But they would leave on Saturday morning. What would he do then?

"Dad, do I have to stay around the A-frame always?" whined Bob.

"Now, Bob, it's not as if I'm punishing you for something you did wrong."

Bob wondered what the difference was. The results were the same. He said nothing.

Dr. Duncan came over and sat beside Bob. "Son, I'm making you stay near the A-frame because I love you and want to make sure nothing happens to you. It's my responsibility to protect you. When there is something that might be dangerous, I want you *near* me so that I *can* protect you."

Bob looked at his dad. He loved his dad. Bob loved him because he always tried to do the right things. Bob knew that right now staying around the A-frame was the right thing to do, even if it meant he couldn't go looking for deer in the woods. Bob smiled a little. "How long do you think the prowler will be around here?"

"Not long, I hope," said Dad, hugging his son. "Not long."

The next morning Bob and his dad packed a picnic lunch, got in the car, and drove over to pick up Uncle Joe. Dad wanted to check on the eagles that Ranger Peak had told him about, and Bob and Uncle Joe were going into the Big Pines.

"What's the whistle for, sonny?" asked Uncle Joe as he climbed into the car.

"It's in case I see the prowler," said Bob.

"Good idea," said Uncle Joe, glancing at Dr. Duncan.

If you could take a boat across the lake, the Big Pines were only a short distance away. But ever since Hazel and Ernie had been nesting on Eagle Island, both Dr. Duncan and Uncle Joe rarely used their motorboats. Most of the time they rowed when they were near the island. Uncle Joe didn't mind. He used his boat only for fishing. He felt the motor frightened the fish away.

Driving to the Big Pines was not easy. The road that led to the far end of the lake was little more than two ruts. After being bounced around in the back seat for what seemed like a long time, Bob could finally see the tall trees of the Big Pines.

"Here we are," said Dad, stopping the car. "If there are eagles around here, they would be over on the other side. You two probably want to get out here and go into the Big Pines. I'll go

on and check for eagles, and then come find
you. I should be back in an hour or so."

Bob and Uncle Joe got out of the car, and
Dad continued on down the road. Bob ran up
a small hill and looked into the Big Pines.

"Wow! I always forget how really big they are,"
he muttered to himself. The pine needles far
above his head sang a soft, breathy song in the
breeze.

Bob sat down to wait for Uncle Joe. At one
time Uncle Joe's ancestors had owned all the
land around Ward's Lake. It was in the Big
Pines that Uncle Joe's great-great-grandfather
had built his home. It was the first house built
by white men anywhere near Ward's Lake.

"Well, they haven't changed any, have they, sonny?" Uncle Joe was beside Bob, looking into the small valley that contained the Big Pines. "Nope, they haven't changed in many a year," said Uncle Joe, answering himself as he walked down the hill.

Bob followed. It was not that the trees were a different kind. White pines grew all over Waunakee National Forest. These were just bigger—much bigger.

"Will the other trees ever get this big?" asked Bob.

"Maybe so," said Uncle Joe, looking up at the sun coming through the pine needles over a 125 feet away. "But it's going to take a long time—a real long time."

"How old are these trees?"

"See that big one over there?" Uncle Joe pointed to the biggest tree in the area. It was over three and a half feet wide at the bottom. "Some scientists were up here studying these trees a few years back. They said that one is about 275 years old."

"How do they know?"

"They took a drill and bored a hole in it and counted the rings on the strip of wood that came out. I watched them do it." Uncle Joe put his hand on the rough bark of the giant pine.

"Way back when George Washington was president, this tree was as big as the trees around my cabin. Big pines like these are real special."

"Why aren't there big trees like these in other places?"

"Cut them all down," answered Uncle Joe as he turned to walk along a faint path. "There was a time when all of Michigan and most of the rest of the states around here were covered with white pines as big as these. But they needed them for lumber, so they cut them down."

Bob walked quietly beside Uncle Joe, hoping he would go on talking. He did. "Only a few spots in the whole country still have white pines like these. It's because of these pines that the government wanted to get this land into the national forest. And it's because of these pines that I sold them the land. After me there won't be any more Wards to take care of them. So I gave the job to Uncle Sam and his forest rangers."

"Are these the biggest trees in the world?" asked Bob.

"Oh, no, sonny. Out in California whole forests of redwood trees grow that are three times bigger than these pines. And there are some white pines that are bigger, but not much bigger."

Bob knew that Uncle Joe was going to a little graveyard on the side of one of the hills. Uncle Joe would pull some weeds from along the iron fence that surrounded the graveyard, and then dust some pine needles off the grave markers of his ancestors.

"These pines are here because my great-grandmother didn't want the trees around her house cut down. They were up here cutting down every tree they came to. But she wouldn't let them cut down her pines. That was over a hundred years ago, young man."

Soon they passed the place where Uncle Joe's grandmother's home had once stood. The building had crumbled away a long time ago. But the stone fireplace was still there. The chimney had fallen a few years ago, but the hearth was still in place.

"What's this?" Uncle Joe asked as he came to the old fireplace. Bob ran around Uncle Joe and stopped. Someone had stacked the rocks from the fallen chimney and made a low wall up against the back of the hearth. There was a large bed of pine needles up against the wall.

"Has someone been sleeping here?" asked Bob.

"Looks like it. Cooking here too, it seems," said Uncle Joe as he stooped to pick up an empty tin can. "Humm. Looks like it's our tennis-shoe boy." He pointed to a shoeprint in dried mud.

"Do you think he's here now?" asked Bob, looking around.

"Judging by the rust on this can and the dried footprint, I'd say he's not been here in a while."

Honk! Honk! Honk!

"That's our car! Why's Dad back so soon? And what's he honking about?"

8 Mrs. Howard

By the time Bob and Uncle Joe had reached the edge of the Big Pines, Dr. Duncan was there also. "Sorry to cut your day up here short," said Dad. "Ranger Peak just called me on the radio. Seems that they have found some things they think may belong to us."

In the car on the way to George's Grocery and Bait Shop, Dad explained. The National Forest Service had hired some men to remove old buildings from the new area of the Waunakee National Forest. They had been bulldozing the buildings of the Smiths' farm when they found some things.

"What kinds of things?" asked Bob.

"Our cooler, for one thing," answered Dad. "And some of Joe's tools, he thinks. Dick wants us to come and identify what belongs to us."

"Did he say anything about finding a person there?" asked Uncle Joe.

"No. But he did say he was sure some of what he found was not ours."

"Like what?" asked Bob.

"We'll know pretty soon," said Dad.

As they drove past the Smiths' farm, they saw the bulldozer. It was stopped halfway through the house.

When they arrived at the store, George Collier showed them into a small back room. Ranger Peak was there along with the man who drove the bulldozer.

"Is any of this yours?" asked Ranger Peak, pointing to the things spread out on the table.

"That's our cooler," answered Dr. Duncan, looking at the bent lid.

"Listen, I'm sorry about that," said the bulldozer driver. "But I had no idea anything was in that old house. I was just told to knock it down and haul off the big pieces. I didn't know there was anything in the place."

"Any damage is not your fault," said Ranger Peak. "Is any of this other stuff yours?"

"That's my hatchet," said Uncle Joe. "There's my *JW* on the handle. And that's my knife."

"And here's your dipper," said Bob.

Uncle Joe identified several other things, a few of which he did not even know were missing. Also on the table was George Collier's fishing tackle. There were other things too—things like clothes, a pocket watch, cans of food, a fork and spoon, a can opener, soap, and a toothbrush.

"Looks like someone was setting up housekeeping in the place," said Dr. Duncan.

"Any idea who?"

"After you and Joe told me about your prowler and the things that were missing, I contacted the police. I wanted to see if they had any idea who might be around here doing this," answered Ranger Peak. "The description of the boy you gave me fits a runaway from Catawba."

Dr. Duncan looked at Ranger Peak. "Remember I told you that Ralph Howard had died?" asked Ranger Peak. "Well, it seems his wife and son were moving to Lansing."

"Son? I didn't know they had a son," said Dr. Duncan.

"Adopted. An older boy," said the ranger as he looked at some notes he had written on his pad. "He is fourteen and his name is John. His parents were killed in an auto accident when he was six. He then spent four years in different foster homes before the Howards adopted him."

Ranger Peak turned a page of his note pad and went on. "He lived four years with the Howards, and according to all reports was quite happy. He was doing well in school. Then Ralph developed cancer and died. Millie Howard and the boy were going to move to Lansing, where she had a job lined up. But the night before they were to leave, John ran away."

"How long ago was that?" asked Dr. Duncan.

"He's been missing three weeks," said Ranger Peak, closing his note pad.

"Are you sure this stuff belongs to him?" asked George Collier.

"We'll know pretty soon. The police are bringing Mrs. Howard here from Catawba," said Ranger Peak.

"Catawba? She didn't go to Lansing?" asked Dr. Duncan.

"I guess she decided not to go without the boy," said Ranger Peak.

"Probably thought he would settle down, think things through, and come back," said Dr. Duncan.

"I hear car doors out front," said Bob.

Soon Mr. Collier was showing two policemen and Mrs. Howard into the back room. She was a small, thin, middle-aged woman who stood very straight. She wore a pretty green dress with a bow at the neck. She reminded Bob of one of the teachers at his school.

Mrs. Howard looked at the things spread on the table. "Yes, those are John's clothes. And that was my husband's watch." She swallowed hard and blinked her eyes to keep back the tears. "But I don't recognize most of these things."

"Most of them belong to these people," said Ranger Peak, pointing to Uncle Joe, George Collier, and the Duncans.

"I guess John stole them, didn't he? I have never known him to steal anything. I'll pay for anything that he has damaged." She was looking at the cooler.

"I don't think that will be necessary, Mrs. Howard," said Dr. Duncan as he glanced at the others. They nodded.

"Did he steal the watch?" asked one of the policemen.

"No, Ralph gave that to John. It had belonged to my husband's father and meant a great deal to him. Giving it to John was one of the last things that Ralph did." Tears slipped from Mrs. Howard's eyes. She opened her purse and found a tissue. George Collier offered her a chair, and she sat down. Everyone was quiet for a moment. Then Mrs. Howard asked, "Does anyone know where he is?"

"We don't know where he is right now. When we found these things, he was not with them. These people believe they have caught glimpses of him," said Ranger Peak, pointing to Uncle Joe and the Duncans.

"Is he all right?" asked Mrs. Howard.

"The boy we saw seemed to be. At least he was able to run pretty fast," said Dr. Duncan with a smile.

Mrs. Howard opened her purse and brought out a couple of pictures of her son. They all looked at them.

"That looks like the guy we saw the other night," said Bob.

"He's got the same hair color," said Dr. Duncan.

"He's been here at the store a couple of times. Bought some canned food and some bread and peanut butter just a few days ago," added George Collier.

"John couldn't have had much money with him when he left. Probably only about thirty dollars," said Mrs. Howard.

"Is this your husband?" asked Uncle Joe, pointing to one of the pictures. Mrs. Howard nodded. "Then I think I recognize the boy," said Uncle Joe. "Didn't he and your husband come up here to hunt a few years ago? I think I remember giving them permission to hunt on my land."

"It was four years ago. It was their first
hunting trip together, and they loved it. It was
on that trip that they really got to know each
other. I might have guessed that John would
come here. After Ralph died, John spoke of
how much he had enjoyed hunting and fishing
with Ralph. He even spoke of the trip when
they came to a lake near here." Mrs. Howard
bit her lip.

"If he came here because he loved the place,
he's probably still around here," said Dr.
Duncan, looking at Ranger Peak.

"We will notify the people around here and
show them copies of his picture," said one of

the policemen. "We'll ask them to contact us if they see him."

"Mrs. Howard," said Dr. Duncan, "if your son stays around here, it is quite possible that we will be seeing him again. It might help if we knew more about him. Do you know why he ran away?"

"After the funeral I began to make arrangements to find work at a new job. I couldn't run the farm. You see, I was brought up in the city and knew nothing about farming. And neither did John, really. I had friends in Lansing who helped me to find a job there." Mrs. Howard looked at the things on the table, and then went on.

"John helped me pick out the apartment in Lansing. He seemed to like it. We visited the school he would go to in the fall. He said it was a nice school. He helped me with the packing. But then, the night before we were to leave, he ran away."

Mrs. Howard clutched her purse. "He left a note. It said he did not want to move to Lansing. He said he had lived in cities all his life, but now he wanted to stay in the country. He never told me that. He must have been holding it inside, and I was too busy and too upset to notice."

"Sounds like he got upset at the last minute and didn't know what to do, so he ran away," said George Collier.

"When it came down to it, John didn't want to leave Catawba because it was here that he and my husband were so happy," said Mrs. Howard. "I should have paid more attention to him and what he was trying to tell me by talking of all the good times he and my husband had while they were hunting together. But . . ." Mrs. Howard swallowed hard.

"Don't blame yourself, Mrs. Howard. If the boy had a problem, he should have talked to you about it," said Dr. Duncan.

"But he didn't. And now he's out there alone in the woods somewhere, and no one can talk to him."

Bob thought about being alone in the woods. It was fun when you could go into the woods and come out whenever you wanted to. But living in the woods because you were running away would not be fun at all. And now that all of John Howard's stuff was gone, what would he do?

9 Stuart McGregor

After the police and Mrs. Howard had left, Dad, Uncle Joe, Ranger Peak, and George Collier decided they should contact each other on the radio if they saw or heard anything of the runaway.

Since George Collier was the only one with a phone, he would be the one to call the police and tell them any news of John Howard.

It was midafternoon before Bob, Dad, and Uncle Joe drove back to the A-frame. "Mom and Stuart are here," said Bob when he saw the small car in the drive.

Stuart McGregor was beside the A-frame, cleaning his bottles and getting ready for tomorrow. Stuart had been studying the water in Ward's Lake at different times of the year. Every other week he came to the lake and collected water. He then tested it to see what was in it.

Stuart was one of Bob's favorite people. Stuart had been on the university's football team. According to Dad, he was "as strong as Samson." Now Stuart was going to school during the day, and at night he was a night watchman at a factory. Mother said that anyone who saw Stuart in his uniform guarding the place would think twice about breaking in.

In spite of his size, Stuart was gentle. Bob loved to wrestle with him. If Stuart didn't want to move, no amount of pulling or pushing by Bob could move him. The trick was who would stop pulling first. There would then be some quick action, and whoever wound up on top won. Bob was sure that Stuart could have wound up on top every time. But he didn't. And the fun was in wrestling, not winning.

In a flying leap, Bob flung himself at Stuart. Stuart caught him, held him up at arm's length, and said, "Well, who is this?"

"Put me down and I'll show you who it is," said Bob, trying to sound mean, but with a grin sneaking across his face.

"Only if you promise to help me clean my bottles."

"I'll only help you with your old bottles if you win."

"A deal!" said Stuart, putting him down.

"It's only a matter of time before you lose," yelled Bob as he tackled Stuart. Stuart let himself fall to the ground, but it was only a matter of time before Bob wound up on the bottom. While holding him down, Stuart told Bob how the bottles were going to sparkle like the sun when Bob had finished cleaning them. "And then you can clean the mud off my car and make it sparkle. And after that . . ."

"You'll have to beat me again if you are going to get me to help you wash your car," grinned Bob from under Stuart.

"No problem, little man," said Stuart, standing up and picking up Bob with him. "When you're done with the bottles,

we'll wrestle over who helps whom with the car."

"Hi, Bob!" called Mom from the back door.

"Just a minute, Stuart." Bob ran to the back door and hugged his mother. Soon he was back, helping Stuart clean his bottles.

At supper that night most of the conversation was about John Howard. "Losing his parents is bad enough," said Mom, "but then to lose a second father just a few years later. . . Sounds like the poor boy has had a hard time."

"But it's never right to steal," said Dad. "The Bible is clear about that."

"I know how torn up you can get on the inside when your father dies," said Stuart. "I was thirteen when my dad died. I went right on, but inside I was mad. I wanted to change things, but I didn't even really know how I wanted them changed."

Bob had never thought of Stuart having a father.

"It's that way whenever someone you love dies," said Dr. Duncan.

Stuart looked out the window. "My dad led me to the Lord when I was eight. I knew he was a Christian and that when he died he went to be with the Lord. But I missed him very much for a long time. I wish I could talk to that kid out there. I'd try to tell him a few things."

"I hope some of us do get a chance to talk to him," said Dad. "I think what he really needs is help from the Lord."

Several heads nodded in agreement. "It was when I gave up trying to change things and asked the Lord to help me that I got things straightened out about my dad," said Stuart.

During family devotions that night everyone prayed for John Howard and his special needs.

The next morning everyone was up before daylight. Bob and Stuart were going to the other end of the lake to fill the bottles. Dad was to be on the deck to watch the morning activity on the eagles' nest as the sun came up. Mom was up to prepare breakfast for everyone. It was still dark when Bob and Stuart went down to the boats.

Bob wanted to row. "The sun's just about to come up," said Stuart, "and I've got to fill a set of bottles at dawn. You'd better let me row out. You can row back, okay?"

"A deal!"

After they rounded the bend in the lake and passed out of sight of the eagles' nest, Stuart started the motor. They swiftly crossed to the far end of Ward's Lake. Stuart stopped the motor near a floating milk bottle that he had anchored there. The milk bottle marked the place where Stuart had been collecting water for his study. They rowed over to the marker.

Stuart let Bob hold the thermometer in the water while he filled the bottles. Then Stuart recorded the temperature and wrote some other notes in his field book. After that they rowed a little ways from the milk bottle, started the motor, and went ashore in the Big Pines. Stuart carefully labeled, sealed, and packed the bottles of lake water in a box. Later, in the laboratory, he would carefully check what was in the lake water.

More bottles would have to be filled at nine o'clock. While they waited, they walked around the Big Pines. Bob showed Stuart the rock wall by the fireplace, the footprint, and the pine-needle bed.

After the nine o'clock bottle filling, they started the motor and headed toward the A-frame. When they came close to the bend in the lake, they turned off the motor, and Bob started rowing. Bob rowed much slower than Stuart, and the boat kept turning this way and that. He also made a lot more noise as he rowed.

"If you keep the oars in the water when you are pulling and don't pick them up so high, you won't make so much noise," said Stuart, smiling. "If you are not careful, you'll frighten away the eagles."

Bob glanced up toward the nest. One of the eagles was looking down at the boat. Bob didn't want to frighten him away. Although he knew that it would take more than noisy rowing to frighten away the eagles, he tried to row more quietly.

That afternoon Dad went with Stuart for more bottle filling. Bob stayed with Mom. Dad had carefully explained the whistle-blowing and that Bob had to stay within sight of the A-frame. Mom wanted to have Bob stay inside for the afternoon, but Dad felt that it would be all right for Bob to go outside as long as Mom always knew where he was.

While Mom cleaned the A-frame, Bob was on the deck. He hoped to see the deer family come to the lake to drink. But they never came. He looked up at the eagles' nest. An eagle was sitting on the nest, doing nothing. There was nothing even to write in his field book.

What could Bob do that would be interesting? Then he remembered the strawberry patch. The people who had owned the A-frame had planted strawberries over by the road. The strawberry patch was grown over with weeds because no one took care of it, but last year Bob had been able to gather some good strawberries.

"Mom, I'm going over to see if there are any strawberries," announced Bob as he passed through the A-frame.

"There probably won't be any ripe. It's too early."

"I'm just going to check." It was better than doing nothing.

"Do you have your whistle?"

"Yes, Mom." Bob went out the back door and headed for the strawberry patch. When he arrived, he couldn't find any ripe ones. But while looking at the ground, he did see something. There in the soft dirt was a tennis-shoe print. Had someone else been looking for strawberries too? Bob looked toward the woods. Then he saw tennis shoes under a sumac bush that grew on the edge of the strawberry patch. These tennis shoes had feet in them!

10 The Sumac Bush

Bob was kneeling in the strawberry patch, looking straight at the sumac bush. Slowly he started to bring his hands up to the whistle on his chest. He touched it.

"Don't you dare blow that whistle!" said the person behind the sumac leaves. Bob was sure it was John Howard. Who else could it be? Bob's heart was pounding rapidly. His mouth was dry. John must have been able to see Bob, but the leaves hid him from Bob.

"Why shouldn't I?" asked Bob. Immediately he thought it was a dumb question.

"Because I don't want anybody to know I'm here. I don't even want you to know I'm here."

"But—but I do." Another dumb remark, thought Bob. After all the talk about John

Howard's special needs, all Bob could do was make dumb remarks. The family had prayed that they would get to talk to John Howard. Here Bob was talking to him and all he could do was say dumb things. Bob prayed silently, "Oh, Lord, help me say the right things."

"Yeah, you do know I'm here, don't you? But now, what am I going to do about it?"

"Your name is John Howard, isn't it?" asked Bob, thinking that would be a good place to start.

"So they were able to figure that out already, huh?"

Bob immediately thought maybe he had done wrong by telling John he knew who he was. It was too late now.

"The police figured out who you were from the clothes and the watch they found at the Smiths' place yesterday," Bob said.

"My watch," John Howard's voice cracked. "They've got my watch, haven't they?"

"Yes." Bob wondered what to say next. "Was it your dad's watch?" There was a long pause. Bob wondered if he had said the right thing. "If it was your dad's watch, . . ."

"Why can't everybody leave things alone?" blurted out John. "I was doing just fine until they came with that bulldozer. Why can't everybody leave me alone? Why don't all of you go away and leave me alone?"

Bob thought it sounded like John Howard was about to cry.

"We can't leave. We belong here," he said.

"You can't belong here. This is government land," John answered.

"The government wants my father to study the eagles over on the island."

There was a pause. "That explains why they haven't torn down that A-frame. They got your dad studying the eagles, huh?"

"Yes."

"And that's why that ranger comes up here all the time, and why they've got that big cop here protecting you. They want you safe while your dad studies the eagles. Don't want you to get hurt by the runaway in the woods, huh?" Now John Howard sounded mean.

"The ranger and my dad are friends. And Stuart is not a cop. He's one of my dad's students."

"Then what's he got that uniform for, if he isn't a cop?"

"What uniform?"

"He's a cop. I saw the hat to his uniform in the back of his car. I'm not dumb. I know a police badge when I see one. They're afraid I might pop out of the woods and hurt you all and mess up the eagle study or something. So they've got a cop up here guarding you. Right? And right now the cop and your dad are out looking for me at the other end of the lake, aren't they? Huh?"

"Stuart is a night watchman at a factory back home," answered Bob. "That's why he's got that uniform. He's not a policeman. He and my dad are out collecting water samples on the other side of the lake for Stuart's study."

"Collecting water samples from the other side of the lake for Stuart's study," mocked John. "Come on. Hand me one I can believe. Why not get lake water right out here if that's what he wants?"

"Stuart's got to collect from the same place all the time or his study won't be any good. And they don't collect the water here because they don't want to disturb the eagles."

"How nice. You don't want to disturb the eagles, so you go to the other side of the lake to get water. Aren't you all sweet!"

"Well, we don't want the eagles to leave."

"Yeah, I bet you don't!"

Bob thought he might have said something he shouldn't have. Better change the subject. "My dad says he'd like to talk to you. He's very good at helping people with problems."

"My biggest problem is him. And I don't want to talk to anybody, especially him and that cop."

"But I told you Stuart's a night watchman, not a cop."

"I don't care if he's a cop at night or a cop during the day. He's still a cop. And the sooner he's out of here, the better I'll like it. In fact, the sooner all of you are gone, the better I'll like it."

"What are you going to do now that they've got all your stuff?" asked Bob.

"Don't worry about me," said John Howard gruffly. "I'll manage just fine if you all will just get out of here."

"We could help you . . ."

"I don't need your help."

"The Lord could help you."

"I—I don't need any help from anybody." The voice cracked. Bob could tell that John Howard was having a hard time again.

"If I blow my whistle, my mom and dad will come and we could . . ."

"Don't blow that whistle! If you blow that whistle, I'll—I'll make you leave. That's what I'll do."

"Bob. Bob, are you all right?" Mother was calling from the deck.

"Tell her you're fine," whispered John Howard. Bob hesitated and looked toward the A-frame. "Tell her you're fine, or you'll wish you had." John sounded desperate.

"I'm fine, Mom," yelled Bob.

"I think you've probably had enough strawberries. You don't want to be sick," called Mom. "Come back over here where I can see you from the deck. Okay, Bob?"

"Tell her 'okay,'" whispered John Howard.

"Okay, Mom," yelled Bob.

"Now listen good, Bob. Don't you tell anybody you've talked to me. If you tell them, they'll start looking around here for me, and then you've had it."

"What would you do?"

"I'd—I'd—I'd burn down your A-frame. I'd kill the eagles. Something. But you'll know."

Bob was frightened. "I won't tell," he whispered.

"You'd better not, kid. If you know what's good for you."

"Bob, are you coming?" called Mom.

"Yes, Mom." Bob's heart was pounding as he walked toward the A-frame.

That night at supper most of the conversation centered on Stuart's study. Bob was just as glad. He didn't feel like talking.

"We're all done, and you've hardly touched your dinner," said Mom, watching Bob fiddle with his food.

"I guess I'm not hungry," answered Bob, putting down his fork.

"Don't you feel well?" asked Mom as she slipped her hand across his forehead.

"I'm fine."

"No fever. It must have been all those strawberries," said Mom.

"There weren't any ripe."

"Well, it sure took you long enough to find that out," said Mom, picking up some of the supper plates and taking them into the kitchen.

"I know what his problem is," said Stuart. "He hasn't been whipped at a wrestling match since yesterday, but I can fix that real fast."

"I don't feel like wrestling tonight."

"You don't want to wrestle? Something is ailing the boy," said Stuart, leaning back in his chair.

"Something's ailing him all right," said Dad. "But I don't think it's that he's sick. I think there's something on his mind. Want to talk about it, son?"

To say there was nothing on his mind would be a lie. "I don't want to talk about anything, Dad." That was the truth, but Dr. Duncan read through what was said.

"Okay, son. Maybe later."

Dad stood up. "Stuart, how about building a fire? The rain has made it a little damp and cool in here."

Stuart built a fire while Dad helped Mom clear the dishes from the table. Bob sat in the big chair across from the sofa and looked at nothing.

"Let's have devotions by the fire tonight," suggested Mom.

They all sat by the fireplace.

After Dad read the Bible, they all prayed. Bob's prayer was very short. It was the only one which did not mention John Howard. Bob decided he might say something he didn't want to say if he prayed for John Howard. He would pray for him later.

After devotions Dad and Stuart talked while Mom washed the dishes and Bob stared at the fire. Later Mom held up a plastic bag filled with trash. "Someone needs to take out the garbage," she sang, looking at Bob.

"Sure, Mom," said Bob. He stood up and then stopped. Bob became very frightened as he thought of going to the trash can alone.

"I think we'd better have Stuart take out the trash tonight," said Dad as he looked at Bob's face. "And Stuart, let me give you a couple of locks to put on the trash can."

"Old Randal been getting the clips off?" asked Stuart.

"No," answered Dad. "But there may be someone else interested in our trash tonight."

Try as he might, Bob could never hide anything from Dad. But he had kept his promise. He hadn't said anything. Dad just knew, somehow.

11 Bob's Decision

"Bob! Bob, get up. Your mother and Stuart are about to leave," called Dad. It was still dark. Bob crawled slowly out of bed. Today was not at all like yesterday. Yesterday he had been eager to get up early. But he wished that today had never come. Not that Mom and Stuart's leaving was bad. Mom would be back tomorrow, and Stuart would be back in a couple of weeks. It was everything else he dreaded.

Bob sat on the edge of his bed. He had not slept well. Normally rain put him to sleep. But last night the rain on the roof seemed like drums beating to keep him awake.

"Bob! Aren't you going to come and say good-by?" called Mom.

"I'm coming as soon as I get dressed." Bob went over to the chair near the door and picked up his clothes. As he started putting them on, he could hear his parents.

"Are you sure he shouldn't go back with me?" asked Mom. "I don't think he's sick, but there is something wrong with him. And that John Howard fellow is out there somewhere. Stuart said he saw fresh tennis-shoe tracks near the cars this morning. I'm a little worried."

"I think Bob's safe here. And, frankly, I might need him," said Dad. Normally Bob would have felt good to have heard his father say that. But right now Bob didn't know how he felt. "Besides, there are a few things that I think our son needs to learn. Running away won't help him to learn them."

Bob wondered what Dad meant by that.

"Maybe I should call down and tell them I can't be at the Women's Missionary Circle dinner tonight. Then I could stay here with you," said Mom.

"You're the president, and this is the last big event of the year. There is no good reason for you not to be there," answered Dad. "Then after tomorrow morning's church service, you can drive back up here. You'll be here tomorrow night. Besides, I think it would be best for Bob and me to settle a few things sort of man to man."

"Man to man," thought Bob. That usually meant something that was good for him but not necessarily a whole lot of fun. Bob had his clothes on. He opened the door.

"Ah, Bob. Just in time to help your mother carry a couple of things out to the car. Then I'm sure Stuart could use some help with his bottles."

"Yes, Dad."

In a few minutes the good-bys had been said, and Stuart drove off in his car, followed by Mom in the Duncans' car. Bob sat down to the breakfast that had been left for him. Dad went out to watch the eagles. The rain had ended and a beautifully clear day was dawning.

Bob did not eat much of the breakfast. To him the day seemed gloomy.

"Bob," called Dad throught the door to the deck. "When you've finished your breakfast, I want you to come out here."

"Yes, Dad." Since there was going to be no putting it off, he might as well go and get it

over with. Bob couldn't see how this mess was
going to end well. Either he was going to talk
to Dad, which would mess everything up, or he
was not going to tell Dad anything, which
would not please Dad at all. What should he
do?

When Bob went out onto the deck, his
father was looking through the telescope.
"Come on over and sit down, son. If my figures
are right, there ought to be some big doings in
the eagles' nest any day now."

Bob looked at Hazel and Ernie through his
binoculars. Things seemed to be just like usual
to him. Hazel was sitting on the eggs, and
Ernie was standing on the edge of the nest.

"Now, Bob, this is the way I see it. You met someone around here yesterday. Stuart and you were together all morning, and Mom says the only time you were out of her sight was when you went to pick strawberries. She says you stayed over there for a little while, and you said that no strawberries were ripe yet."

Dad paused to write something in his field book. Bob already felt cornered. Dad could figure out almost anything.

Dad looked straight at Bob. "I think you were talking to someone over there by the strawberry patch. Were you?" Bob said nothing. He looked at the wooden floor of the deck.

"Bob, I *am* your father. You know that the Bible tells you to obey your parents, don't you?" asked Dad without raising his voice, but in a way that let Bob know he meant business.

"Yes, sir." Bob had a lump in his throat.

"One of the ways you obey your parents is by answering questions they ask you, isn't it?"

"Yes, sir." The lump was growing.

"Bob, I asked you if you had talked to anyone by the strawberry patch yesterday." No one said anything. A tear fell onto the deck in front of Bob. "Bob, did he make you promise not to tell that you and he had talked?" It was hard for Bob to breathe. "Bob, did he threaten you? Did he say he was going to hurt you if you told us he was here?"

How could Bob say anything? If he told Dad about what happened yesterday, John Howard would burn the A-frame, or kill the eagles, or something. His jaw trembled and more tears fell onto the deck.

"Bob, look at me." Bob raised his head and looked at his father.

"Bob, the Bible tells Christians to witness to other people about God's love. We are to tell sinners that Christ died on the cross to pay the punishment for their sins. Isn't that true?"

Bob nodded. Why was Dad talking to him about witnessing?

"Now, son, let's say that somebody told me that I should not tell anyone about God's plan of salvation. Let's say that the person says he will lock me up in prison or kill me if I witness. Now, Bob, whom should I obey—God or that person?"

"God," whispered Bob.

"Yes. I am to obey God, because He is a higher authority than any man."

"But, what if—" Bob stopped.

"What if what, son?"

"If you told the man you wouldn't witness to anybody, then you'd be breaking your word if you did."

"Bob, it would have been wrong of me to have told the man that I wouldn't witness for Christ. I would have been setting myself in a place where I would have to disobey God to keep my word. I shouldn't do that. It's not right."

"But—but what if he made you—and you did?" sobbed Bob.

"Oh, Bob," said Dad as he gently put his arm around his son's shoulders. "Bob, I have to do what's right no matter what. If I have done wrong, first I have to ask God to forgive me, and then I have to do what's right from then on."

It all seemed so easy when Dad said it. Why did everything have to get in such a mess?

"It's hard, isn't it, son?" Bob nodded. "Remember the first night we were up here this week? We read that 'they that wait upon the Lord shall renew their strength; they shall mount up with wings as eagles.' " Bob nodded again.

"You know how easy it looks for Hazel and Ernie to fly? They fly because they are supposed to fly. God made them that way.

Christians are supposed to do what's right, because God made us that way. When we do what's right, God will strengthen us so that we can keep doing what's right."

All Bob could do was to trust the Lord and his dad. He would ask the Lord to forgive him, and then ask his dad to help him work things out somehow. Bob turned his head in toward his dad's chest. "I did talk to someone yesterday," he muttered. There. He had started. He felt better.

Whurr. Whurr. Whurr-rr-rr-rr. . .

Someone was starting their motorboat. Bob sat up. Dad used his binoculars to look down at the lake. "Is that who you talked to?"

Bob looked toward the dock. "Yes, sir."

"I wonder where he thinks he's going? You can't get off the lake in a boat. Bob, do you know where he's going?"

"No, sir."

"He's headed toward Eagle Island." Dad glanced at the eagles' nest. The eagles were watching the motorboat far below them.

"Oh, Dad, the eagles. I think he's going to kill the eagles. He said he would if I told anyone he was here."

"He had no way of knowing you said

anything to me. Why would he want to kill the eagles?"

"If they are not here, we have to leave."

"You told him that?"

"I didn't mean to."

"And he thinks if we are not here all his problems would be over. How is he going to kill the eagles, Bob?"

"I don't know."

"It doesn't look like he's got anything with him in the boat."

Trees blocked the view of the shore of Eagle Island. Dad ran down the steps from the deck, followed by Bob. They ran to a place where they could watch as John Howard beached the boat on Eagle Island. John Howard looked up at the eagles' nest and then over at the A-frame. He reached back, picked up a gas can, and jumped out of the boat.

"He's going to try to burn the island," said Dad, putting down his binoculars. "Bob, call Uncle Joe and tell him John Howard's burning Eagle Island. Then call George Collier and Ranger Peak. Don't leave the radio until they know what's going on."

Dr. Duncan ran toward the tiny rowboat. Bob was looking through his binoculars at the island. John Howard disappeared into the bushes of the island. Bob looked up at the eagles. They were watching John Howard cross their island.

"Bob, call them *now*!" yelled Dad. Bob ran toward the A-frame.

12 Eagle Island

As he ran, Bob prayed, "Lord, forgive me—and help me." It wasn't a long prayer, but Bob knew the Lord knew what he meant. He also knew the Lord would answer him.

"Uncle Joe. Calling Uncle Joe. Mr. Collier. Ranger Peak. This is Eagle Watch. Come in, please." No answer. He tried again. No answer. Where were they?

"This is Bob of Eagle Watch, calling Uncle Joe, Mr. Collier, or Ranger Peak. Come in, please."

After a short pause, Uncle Joe answered. "Bob, this is Joe. What's going on? Over."

"John Howard's on Eagle Island, and he's going to burn it. Over."

"Where's your father? Over."

"He's going over to the island in our rowboat. Over."

"How do you know the boy's going to burn the island? Over."

"He took the gas can from the boat. Over."

"After the rain we had last night, nothing over on the island is going to burn. But gas on wet leaves is going to make a lot of smoke. Over."

"What about the eagles? Over."

"Now that's another matter. No bird likes smoke around its nest. I'm going to get in my boat and ride over there. Your dad may need some help with that boy. Do either of them have a gun? Over."

"Dad doesn't. I don't know about John Howard. Over."

"I'd better put mine in the boat, just in case. I'm on my way. Over and out."

Bob wanted to go and see if he could see anything on Eagle Island. He glanced out the window at Hazel and Ernie. They were both in the nest, looking down at things on the island. Bob wanted to see what was happening. But Dad had given him other things to do.

"This is Bob of Eagle Watch calling George Collier or Ranger Peak. Come in, please."

"This is George. I heard everything you told Joe Ward. I'm calling the National Forest Headquarters to get ahold of Ranger Peak. Then I'll call the police. After that I'll close up the store and get there as soon as I can. Anything else I should do, Eaglet? Over."

"Not that I know of. But my name is Bob. Over and out." Immediately Bob wondered if he had been rude. Too late now.

"I'll be there as soon as I can, Bob. Out."

Maybe *asking* Mr. Collier to call him Bob would have been okay. Bob was sure that telling him like that could not have been good. But he had other things to worry about now.

Bob ran down to the shore of Ward's Lake. From there he could see all of one side of Eagle Island. Both boats were beached on the island. Using his binoculars, Bob was able to see his father through the trees. He was climbing toward the top of the hill which made Eagle Island. Then he disappeared on the other side of the island.

At that moment John Howard ran around the other end of the island. He knelt down, lit a match, and threw it on the ground a little ways from him. Nothing happened. The match went out.

John picked up a stick and tried to light it with another match. After several tries, it started to burn. He stuck it toward the area where he had thrown the match. Gasoline fumes caught fire and started making flames and smoke.

The flames spread along the narrow path where he had poured gasoline. John Howard stood breathing heavily and looking at the flames and the smoke.

Bob saw his father come over the top of the hill behind John. Dad must have shouted something because John turned and looked at him. Dr. Duncan started walking slowly toward him.

John Howard appeared to be listening to Dr. Duncan because he kept shaking his head. Then Dr. Duncan kept walking toward the tall, blond teenager. John would turn, run a few steps, grab onto a tree, and stand behind it. Dr. Duncan kept slowly walking.

Finally they were at the same tree. Dr. Duncan reached out and touched John Howard. John held on to the tree as if he were about to fall over. He nodded his head.

Smoke was still rising from the flames.

Dr. Duncan looked up at the eagles' nest. Bob did too. Both eagles were still there, looking down at the two people on their island. Then one eagle looked out across the lake. Bob saw Uncle Joe's motorboat come around the bend of the lake, heading toward Eagle Island.

Bob looked back at his father and John Howard. Dr. Duncan was talking to John. Smoke was billowing across the island.

Bob wanted to shout to his father, but he knew he would not hear. Why wasn't he putting out the fire? Didn't he even care about the eagles? No bird likes smoke around its nest. Uncle Joe had said so. What if Hazel and Ernie left? Bob wanted Dad to stop talking to this runaway who made all this mess and start fixing things up before it was too late.

Dr. Duncan and John Howard began to walk toward the narrow strip of flames that now stretched around the end of Eagle Island. They began picking up large handfuls of wet leaves and throwing them on the burning places—putting out the fire.

KABOOM!

Dr. Duncan pushed John Howard to the ground and threw himself over the boy. The fire had reached the gas can, and it had exploded. Dirt, leaves, and branches splashed into the water.

"Kee-Yelp! Kee-Yelp! Kee-Yelp!" called Hazel and Ernie as they flew across the lake.

"No!" thought Bob. "Too late. Everything is too late."

13 John Howard

In the A-frame Uncle Joe sat on the chair across from the sofa. John Howard sat on one end of the sofa. He looked thin and tired as he sat stooped over with his arms hanging straight between his legs. On the table beside him was an untouched sandwich that Dr. Duncan had made for him. It had been about an hour since the explosion on Eagle Island.

Bob was on the deck. His father and Ranger Peak had gone over to inspect the damage done to Eagle Island. Mr. Collier had gone back to his store to guide the police and Mrs. Howard to the A-frame. Bob glanced at the empty eagles' nest. He opened his field book, recorded the date and the time, and then wrote, "Explosion on Eagle Island. Hazel and Ernie left." He closed the book.

Bob turned to go into the A-frame when his father and Ranger Peak started rowing back from the island. Bob saw John Howard. He was the reason for all this trouble—the reason the eagles' nest was empty. Bob had not spoken to John Howard since he, Dad, and Uncle Joe had come from the island. Bob had not been able to think of anything to say. His father had done most of the talking, telling John Howard that everything would be all right. How could Dad say that? The eagles were gone.

Bob could hold it in no longer. "You said you would do something *if* I told that you were here, but you went out to burn the island anyway."

John Howard looked at Bob for a moment, and then back down at the floor.

"Why?" demanded Bob. "Why do you have to go and mess things up for other people? Just because things are messed up for you?"

John looked at Bob again. "You wouldn't understand," he muttered.

"Why didn't *you* leave?" demanded Bob. "You were the one who didn't belong here. Why didn't you just go to Lansing with your mother?"

John Howard did not respond.

"She said you liked the apartment, and that the school was . . ."

"How do you know I liked the apartment?"

"Your mother told us."

"When?"

"When she came here to identify your stuff at George's grocery."

"How did she get here?"

"The police brought her from Catawba."

"Catawba? Not Lansing?"

"She didn't go to Lansing without you."
John Howard looked down.

"See," said Bob, "you mess things up for
everybody." Bob was mad, and he felt as if he
were attacking his enemy and winning.
"Why do you have to run around messing
things up all the time?"

"You wouldn't understand," said John,
looking at the floor. "You have a good dad."

Bob was shocked. For the first time he
thought of himself in John Howard's place.
Bob did have a dad, a dad whom he loved and
who loved him. But John didn't. Even if the
eagles' nest were empty and they had to leave
Ward's Lake forever, Bob still had his dad.
They could go somewhere else together. But
John Howard didn't have a dad to go
anywhere with.

"Son," said Uncle Joe, trying to change the
subject, "why don't you eat that sandwich?"

John looked at it. "I'm not hungry."

Bob knew that John had to be hungry. He
probably had had nothing to eat since they had
found his stuff at the Smiths' place. But Bob
understood. Sometimes you could be starving
but not feel like eating.

Bob felt sorry for John Howard, and he felt

sorry for the things he had just said and how he had said them. How could you help a person if you were mad at him? And helping people is what Christians are supposed to do. Now Bob was messing things up.

"Lord," Bob prayed silently, "forgive me, and help me to do what's right."

"John," said Bob, "I'm sorry about what I said."

"Said about what?"

"About your messing things up for everybody."

"Well, it's true. I do. I mess things up for me and everybody else."

"But you can always get things straightened out."

"You can, maybe. But you're not in as big a mess as I am."

"No mess is too big for God," answered Bob. John looked at him, but then looked away.

"If we really want to straighten things out and really want to do what's right, God will give us the strength to do it," said Bob. "It may seem hard at first, but God wants us to do what's right. When we do what's right, God gives us the strength so that it will be as easy for us as flying is for . . . for eagles."

John Howard did not understand. And Bob knew that he did not understand. It was so difficult to explain to someone. But Bob didn't know what else to say.

"Bob is right, John," said Dr. Duncan as he and Ranger Peak came in from the deck. "Human beings always seem to be doing things wrong and messing things up. We not only mess things up for other people, but we also sin against God. In our own strength there is no way that we can straighten out that mess. Only God, through the Lord Jesus Christ, can straighten out the problem of sin."

Dr. Duncan walked over and sat on the arm of the sofa near John Howard. "And only when sin is forgiven by God will He give you the strength and wisdom to straighten out your life."

"I—I want to, but, I—Things are in such a mess."

"John, wanting to get things right is the first step. God will work all things out for the best, if we but let Him."

"Humm," said Ranger Peak, looking out the sliding glass door.

"What is it?" asked Dr. Duncan.

"A deer family has come down for a drink on the other side of the lake."

Bob ran to the door and put his binoculars to his eyes. He could see the buck, the doe, and the fawn clearly. Between drinks they looked up and down the lake to make sure that there was no danger approaching. The rest of the people in the A-frame had gathered at the door to look at the deer. Even John Howard had come to see them.

"Do you want to borrow my binoculars?" asked Bob as he removed the strap from his neck and offered the binoculars to John.

"Thanks."

Bob smiled. John looked at Bob with a faint, embarrassed smile. Then he looked at the deer through the binoculars.

Bob glanced at the empty eagles' nest. "Oh, Lord," he prayed silently, "work out this mess. Please."

14 Eaglet

While they were looking at the deer, the police and Mrs. Howard came. Mrs. Howard cried when she saw John. Bob could tell that John was fighting tears too.

Dr. Duncan told them about what had happened that morning. The police asked dozens of questions and wrote notes about everything. Even John answered some of them.

Then Bob asked the one question that seemed to be the most important, but the one that nobody had asked. "Why did you run away in the first place?"

"'Cause she was moving to Lansing."

"What's wrong with Lansing?" asked Bob.

"What's right about it?"

"You never told me you didn't want to go to Lansing," said Mrs. Howard. "We could have worked something out."

"I—I guess I should have told you. But I don't know. It's just that Lansing is so far away from here."

"If Lansing is where the one who loves you is, it's the best place for you," said Dr. Duncan.

"But I wanted to stay up here with the woods and everything. It seems so stupid now."

"It's not stupid, John. I understand," said Mrs. Howard.

"But you have to go to Lansing for that job," said John.

"Who says you have to stay in Lansing all the time?" asked Dr. Duncan. "Bob and I live in a city, but we spend a lot of time in the woods. Ranger Peak and his wife live in the city, but he has a job which keeps him out here in the woods most of the time."

"Maybe you could spend your summers working up here," said Ranger Peak. "In a year or two you would be old enough to get a summer job with the Forest Service. It probably wouldn't be a great job—picking up litter, painting signs, cleaning trash cans, and the like—but you'd be up here in the woods."

"I've had experience with trash cans in these parts," said John.

"I could use someone to help me at the store right now," said George Collier. "So many people up here fishing over at Harris Lake, you know. I've been overrun with business."

"I think it's about time for us to go and see the judge," said one of the policemen.

"The judge?" asked Mrs. Howard.

"Your son has stolen several things, and he has attempted to destroy government property," answered the other policeman.

"He won't have to go to jail, will he?" asked Mrs. Howard.

"We will recommend that he be released in your custody," said the policeman.

"We will not be pressing charges for any of the things that were taken from us," said Dr. Duncan. Uncle Joe and George Collier said they wouldn't either.

"I can't say what the Forest Service will do about the fire over on the island," said Ranger Peak. "But I don't think the fine will be too much."

"Oh, thank you," said Mrs. Howard.

"Thank you," said John Howard. He was fighting tears again.

Dr. Duncan walked over to John Howard. "See, things can get straightened out." Dr. Duncan put his hand on John's shoulder. "John, Bob and I would like to come and talk to you and make sure that things get straightened out all the way."

"Yes." John looked up at Dr. Duncan. "I really need some help."

"Do you think it would be all right for us to come tomorrow afternoon?"

John looked at his mother. She nodded. "Yes. That would be good."

"Good. And maybe after things get settled down a bit, you can come here and spend a few days with Bob and me. We'd like that, wouldn't we, Bob?"

"Sure. And this time you can stay inside instead of outside," said Bob with a smile.

"Thanks," said John Howard.

The policemen and the Howards left. Shortly after that the others left too. As George Collier left, he said, "I'm glad you were around here, Dr. Duncan. You always seem to know how to handle things." Mr. Collier put his hand on Bob's head and messed up his hair.

"And Bob here, he takes after you quite a bit." George Collier winked at Bob as he turned to go to his car. Bob looked at the ground. Mr. Collier did not call him "Eaglet."

After everyone had left, Bob and Dad went out on the deck. "Dad, how can we have John come here to visit us if we have to leave?"

"Why will we be leaving?"

"Well, Hazel and Ernie are gone," said Bob.

"Bob, get your binoculars and look over there." Dad pointed across the lake. Bob could see what he thought was a white eagle head even before he got his binoculars up. It was. It was an eagle.

"They are checking to see if everything is all right now. And look over there on the trees beyond the island. That's probably Hazel."

"Oh, Dad!"

"You see, Hazel and Ernie have a pretty strong tie to the nest right now." Dr. Duncan was looking at the nest through his binoculars. "Look."

Bob looked at the nest and saw a tiny, fluffy white head with a curved yellow beak sticking up. As Bob was watching, Hazel flew over to the nest.

"And here comes Ernie. Looks like he's got a fish," said Dad, looking through his binoculars.

Bob started jumping up and down. "Oh Dad! Dad! Dad!"

"Come on, Bob, stop jumping. You'll go through the deck."

"I can't help it," said Bob, stopping. "I'm so happy."

"Maybe we should pray and thank the Lord for bringing the eagles back," said Dad.

"And for hatching the egg."

"Yes, and for hatching the egg."

"And for John Howard. We need to pray for John Howard."

"Yes, John Howard needs to get saved. I think he's ready. Maybe we can lead him to the Lord tomorrow. And then it's going to take a lot for him to get things straightened out."

"But God will help him 'mount up with wings as eagles.'"

"Yes, He will," smiled Dad. "Just as He's helped you."

"And I need to thank Him for that, too."

While the eagles ate breakfast, both Bob and his dad prayed.